U.S.

COAST GUARD

BY NICK GORDON

BELLWETHER MEDIA · MINNEAPOLIS, MN

EPIC BOOKS are no ordinary books. They burst with intense action, high-speed heroics, and shadows of the unknown. Are you ready for an Epic adventure?

This edition first published in 2013 by Bellwether Media, Inc.

No part of this publication may be reproduced in whole or in part without written permission of the publisher. For information regarding permission, write to Bellwether Media, Inc., Attention: Permissions Department, 5357 Penn Avenue South, Minneapolis, MN 55419.

Library of Congress Cataloging-in-Publication Data

Gordon, Nick.
 U.S. Coast Guard / by Nick Gordon.
   p. cm. – (Epic books: U.S. Military)
 Includes bibliographical references and index.
 Summary: "Engaging images accompany information about the U.S. Coast Guard. The combination of high-interest subject matter and light text is intended for students in grades 2 through 7"–Provided by publisher.
 Audience: Ages 6-12.
  ISBN 978-1-60014-828-6 (hbk. : alk. paper)
 1. United States. Coast Guard–Juvenile literature. I. Title.
 VG53.G6823 2013
 363.28'60973–dc23   2012008560

Text copyright © 2013 by Bellwether Media, Inc. EPIC BOOKS and associated logos are trademarks and/or registered trademarks of Bellwether Media, Inc. SCHOLASTIC, CHILDREN'S PRESS, and associated logos are trademarks and/or registered trademarks of Scholastic Inc.

Printed in the United States of America, North Mankato, MN.

TABLE OF CONTENTS

THE U.S. COAST GUARD

The United States Coast Guard is a branch of the **United States Armed Forces**. It **enforces** laws along U.S. coasts. It also rescues people from disasters at sea.

UNITED STATES COAST GUARD

Founded: 1790

Headquarters: Washington, D.C.

Motto: *Semper Paratus* (Always Ready)

Size: More than 40,000 active personnel

Major Engagements: War of 1812, American Civil War, World War I, World War II, Korean War, Vietnam War, Gulf War, Iraq War, War on Terror

The Coast Guard helps with military **missions** during wartime. Coast Guard members and vehicles support other military branches.

COAST GUARD VEHICLES

ICEBREAKERS

751

U.S. COAST GUARD

COAST GUARD FACT

Cutters are large enough for crews to live on board.

U.S. COAST GUARD

751

Coast Guard ships are called **cutters**. Some cutters do patrol work. Others serve as **icebreakers**.

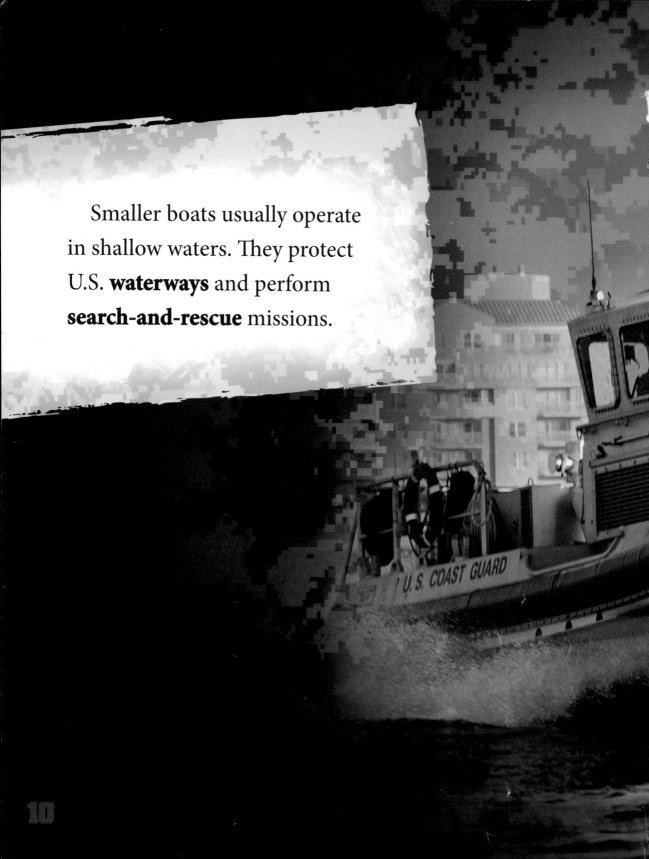

Smaller boats usually operate in shallow waters. They protect U.S. **waterways** and perform **search-and-rescue** missions.

11

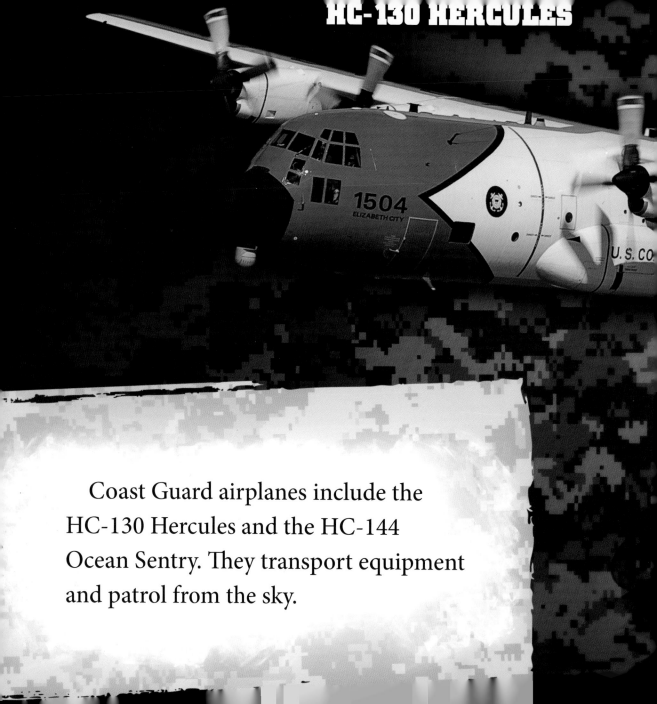

Coast Guard airplanes include the HC-130 Hercules and the HC-144 Ocean Sentry. They transport equipment and patrol from the sky.

HC-144 OCEAN SENTRY

The Coast Guard also uses helicopters. The MH-60 Jayhawk and the MH-65 Dolphin bring **rescue swimmers** to those in need.

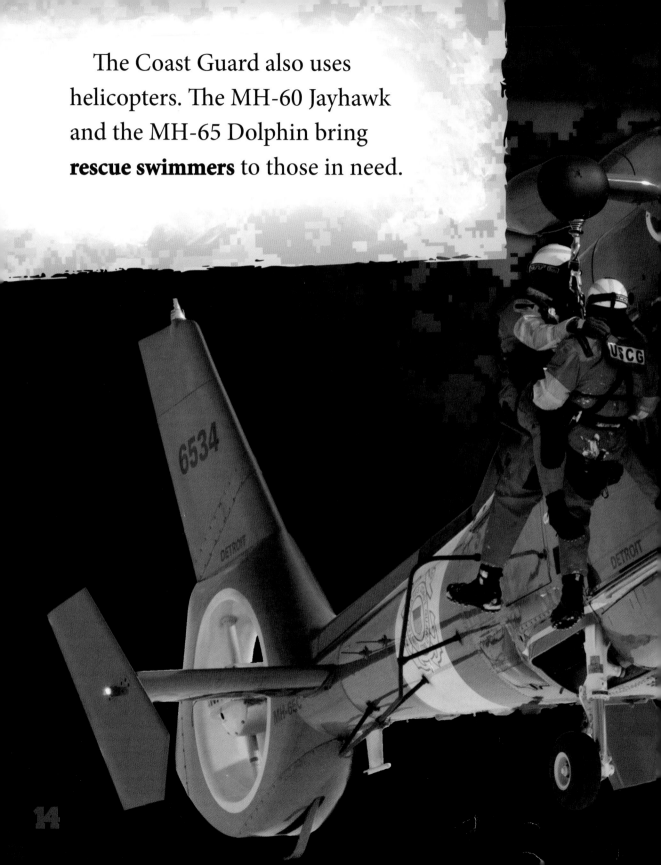

MH-65 DOLPHIN

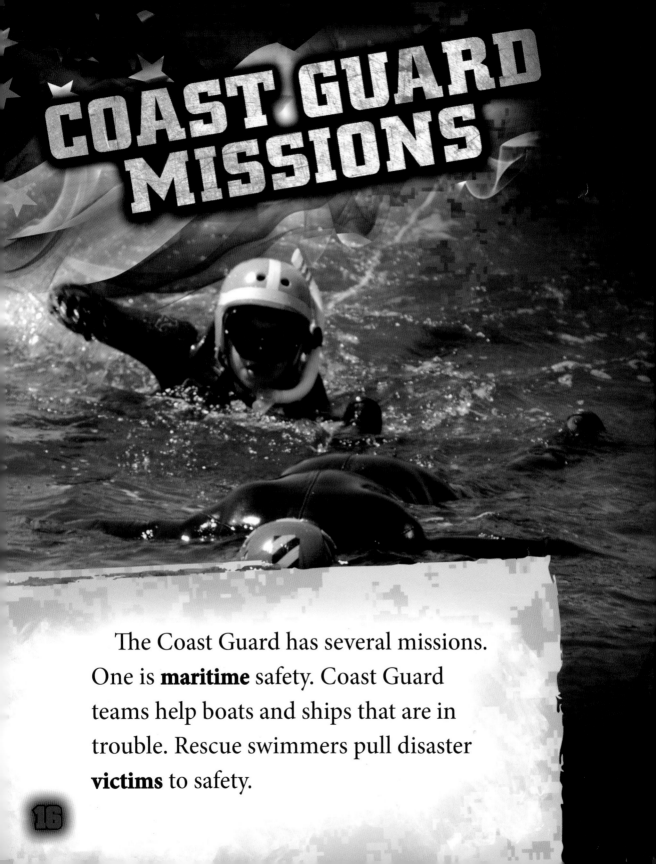

COAST GUARD MISSIONS

The Coast Guard has several missions. One is **maritime** safety. Coast Guard teams help boats and ships that are in trouble. Rescue swimmers pull disaster **victims** to safety.

COAST GUARD FACT

The Coast Guard takes part in around 60 search-and-rescue missions every day.

1331   U.S. COAST GUARD

Another mission is security. Coast Guard ships patrol U.S. coasts. They make sure ships with dangerous or **illegal** materials do not reach the shore.

COAST GUARD FACT

The Coast Guard stops people from entering the U.S. illegally.

Coast Guard members are always ready to help those in need. Their hard work and courage save lives every day.

GLOSSARY

cutters—all Coast Guard ships that are more than 65 feet (20 meters) long

enforces—carries out

icebreakers—large ships that clear paths through ice; the Coast Guard uses icebreakers in the ocean and the Great Lakes.

illegal—not allowed by law

maritime—having to do with the sea

missions—military tasks

rescue swimmers—Coast Guard members trained to rescue people at sea; rescue swimmers leap out of helicopters to save disaster victims.

search-and-rescue—a mission in which someone in a dangerous situation is brought to safety

United States Armed Forces—the five branches of the United States military; they are the Air Force, the Army, the Coast Guard, the Marine Corps, and the Navy.

victims—people who are hurt, killed, or made to suffer

waterways—bodies of water large enough for boat traffic

TO LEARN MORE

At the Library

Braulick, Carrie A. *U.S. Coast Guard Cutters*. Mankato,
Minn.: Capstone Press, 2007.

David, Jack. *United States Coast Guard*. Minneapolis, Minn.:
Bellwether Media, 2008.

Gordon, Nick. *Coast Guard Rescue Swimmer*. Minneapolis,
Minn.: Bellwether Media, 2013.

On the Web

Learning more about the
U.S. Coast Guard is as easy as 1, 2, 3.

1. Go to www.factsurfer.com.

2. Enter "U.S. Coast Guard" into the search box.

3. Click the "Surf" button and you will see a list
of related Web sites.

With factsurfer.com, finding more information
is just a click away.

INDEX